dandelion

dandelion

written and illustrated by gabbie hanna

ATRIA PAPERBACK

New York • London • Toronto • Sydney • New Delhi

This book is dedicated to my Grandma Patty, who saved the newspaper clipping from my very first published poem and gave it to me over a decade later. Thank you for nourishing my love for writing.

Autumn memories rush through my head,
of leaves yellow, orange and red.
Cranberry sauce and pumpkin pies,
cardinals singing and foggy skies.

Tranquil nights and cozy days,
breezes blowing all the ways.
Raking leaves and diving in,
treasured moments with my kin.

Musty air and rustling leaves,
I will cherish these autumn memories.

(Autumn, 2004)

ACKNOWLEDGMENTS

This book has been in the works for about three years by the time it's out of my hands and into yours, and I absolutely could not have made it happen alone.

Dandelion and *Adultolescence* wouldn't be a fraction of what they are without Chance Bone. Years ago, I followed Chance as a fan of his art and somehow convinced him to be my mentor in illustration. Through the years and different projects he's contributed countless ideas and suggestions, pushed me creatively, and inspired me infinitely. He truly breathed life into the pages of this book, and I can't thank him enough for caring as much about this body of work as I do.

This obviously wouldn't have been possible without my team at Simon & Schuster: Daniella Wexler, Loan Le, Isabel DaSilva, and everyone else who worked on this over the last couple of years. Thank you for your patience with me as I wrote, rewrote, re-rewrote, pushed back deadlines, missed those deadlines to write some more, made new ones, and missed them again. Because of your flexibility, I ended up with a version of this book that I was proud to see on shelves (that you procured for me).

Thank you to my agents at CAA, Andrew Graham and Anthony Mattero, for being my biggest fans (if anyone asks) and for dealing with all the scary, complicated contractual stuff so that I could focus on the creative. This process was way easier and more enjoyable with you involved.

Massive thanks to Josh Loveless, my manager, who entered my life in the midst of twenty different deadlines for fifty different projects and somehow juggled them all for me when I was dropping the ball. I don't know how you did that, but if I did, I guess I wouldn't need you so much!

To all my family and friends who encouraged me when I needed it, gave me tough love when I needed it more, and fed me healthy, constructive criticism . . . thank you. I can only imagine that getting weekly texts with stanzas of poetry asking "Does this make sense to you?" gets old after a while, but I appreciate you acting excited, anyway.

I never properly thanked my sisters, Cherisa and Monica, for contributing an illustration each in my last book (Cherisa drew "FLIES," Monica drew "DOLLHOUSE"). I'm so happy I was able to have you be a part of something that was so heavily centered around an experience that only we understand. You both have always inspired me in your different forms of artistry, and your artwork was a beautiful contribution to *Adultolescence*.

Most importantly, to all my fans and supporters of my poetry, music, and other work . . . I couldn't possibly say thank you enough. You are the light in the dark, the silver lining, the reason to keep creating, the reason to keep fighting. Without your support, none of this would matter.

Lastly, to everyone who didn't believe in me or told me I wasn't good enough: thanks a million.

dandelion

BLOOM

i was twenty-six years old when i saw my first flower
and instead of rejoicing in its beauty
i mourned for all the years i was blind

CLAMMY

seashells spray
in disarray
all torn away
    from their other half

but occasionally
if you search patiently
you'll find the anomaly
    of two halves, intact

through tidal waves
and being prey
they find a way
    to stay attached

it gives me faith
in true soul mates
my other half awaits—
    my perfect match

CORDIAL

i broke up with my demons
we're much better off as friends

FLIGHT 141

i don't particularly wish to die
but if this plane chose not to fly
and plummet swiftly from the sky —

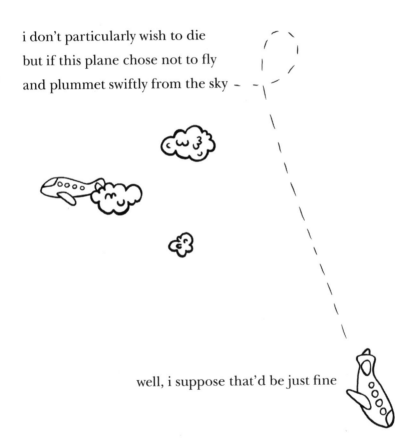

well, i suppose that'd be just fine

4

SOLAR

i'm at the bottom of the universe

when you're on top of the world

BUZZ

one time i watched a fly
fall

and learned no one's perfect,
after all

FORGIVENESS

i don't know if you wonder
and i'm sure you don't care,
but i thought you should know
i don't hate you

anymore

MONEY

if i had a dollar
for every time
a stranger saw me
cry in public
i still couldn't
buy happiness

8

NIGHTLIGHT

daddy! daddy! help me, i'm scared!

> *darling! darling! what's wrong, little girl?*

i'm frightened! i don't like the monster in here!

> *would you like me to check in the closet, my dear,*
> *to make sure it's empty and you're in the clear?*

no, daddy, it's not the closet i fear!
i know there's no monster hiding in there!

> *would you like me to check, then, behind the silk*
> *curtain*
> *just so you know you're alone here for certain?*

daddy, my monster is bigger and worse than
anything hiding behind a silk curtain!

> *daughter, i'll slay this beast that you dread!*
> *i'll banish the monster from under your bed!*

no, daddy, the monster's not under the bed!
i'm scared of the monster that lives in my head!

CLOSET

what is a monster
if not just
an animal
we don't know

HELP

maybe you can't stop world hunger
maybe you can't stop senseless violence

but you can stop loneliness

maybe you can't offer food and water
maybe you can't offer solutions

but you can offer your time

maybe you can't change the past
maybe you can't change the world

but you can change

you can keep your fake care
you can keep your thoughts and prayers

but you can give someone your heart

maybe you can't be a hero
maybe you can't be a savior

but you can be a friend

TINTED

some people dance like no one's watching

i cry hysterically in my car like
no one can see into my window

MURDER

how many times
did you think
you could
kill me
and
get away with it?

FINALLY

summer was
just yesterday
but i've known you for
    a decade

i'm in awe
every single day
at the change in me that
    you made

the love we give
the love we take
is nothing short of
    beautiful

how very exciting
how very excited
i am by you,
    still

EYE

when the world feels calm
and the air is still
the sky will turn to storming

the tides of peace
inevitably change
and often without warn i_{n_g}

ASHAMED

i'm driving home from a thanksgiving meal
late night or early morning—

    highway hypnosis and eerie silence.

i'm forced to suddenly jerk my wheel;
a car stops ahead without warning.

    i blare my horn and disrupt the quiet.

stuffed from stuffing and turkey still,
i find the unwelcome pause unnerving—

    full of dinner and full of impatience.

huffing and judging this driver's skill,
my eyes peel for cause of the swerving—

    i honk again to express my annoyance.

is he drunk? what's wrong with this imbecile?!
my question and blood pressure burning;

    why the hell did he pull over?

i'm now overcome with a shameful chill
my food-filled stomach churning.

    he hands a hungry man his leftovers.

GROSS

tear-stained cheeks
&
drear-stained peaks
&
fear-stained weeks
&
we're-stained freaks

MUTE

the last thing you ever said to me was
"i promise this isn't goodbye"
and i never heard your voice again

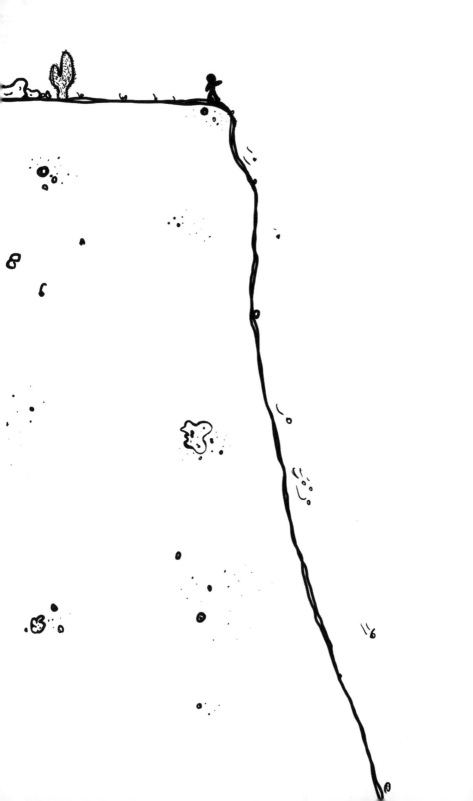

DISTANCE

little by little,
pebble by pebble,
speck by speck of dust—
the mountains eroded
leaving a canyon
between the two of us.

the whispers were bellowed,
resentments were echoed
across a cleft so grand;
all you needed
to close the gap
was to reach out for my hand.

NECRO

i wish you were dead.
not because i hate you,
but because i love you so much.
it's too hard knowing that you're walking around all
breathe-y and pulse-y and not-decompose-y
and i can't have you.
i want your outsides to match my insides.
i want them to be all still and rotting and
soon to be forgotten.

i want to know that the reason you're not calling is
your fingers have turned to dust.
i fantasize that the reason you don't think about me is
the worms have eaten your memory.
it's much kinder to say i can't have your heart
because it no longer beats.
let me down gently.
just die already.

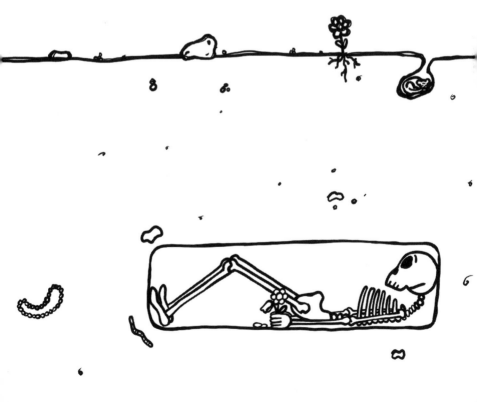

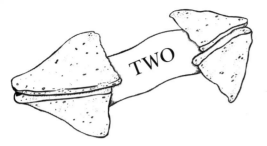

TWO

we were on our second date
circling in the car because
neither of us were ready to go home.
my new home.
empty of furniture.
empty of memories.
i realized:

i have no idea where i am right now.

i live a quarter mile away, but i'm lost.

i don't know these streets.
i don't know these shops.
i'll never know this area less than i know it
right now.

soon,
that random chinese place on the corner that was closed
     when we got there will be my favorite drunk food.
soon,
that donut shop we passed will be my favorite hangover treat.
i'll figure out which gas station has the lowest prices.
i'll choose my favorite grocery store, the one that has the
     best produce.
i'll find my favorite first-date restaurant (thanks to you).

and after that,
i can never unlearn it.
this will be *my* neighborhood.

what a special moment,
to be lost so close to home.

a moment i'll never get back.
a moment i can never recreate.
new, fresh, strange.
not yet mine.

i looked to my left, saw you, and
i realized:

i have no idea where i am right now.

i'm lost.

i don't know you.
i don't know your heart.
i'll never know you less than i know you right now.
i know i'm not ready for love right now,
for love again,
i know i'm just hoping for a distraction.

but what if this is a beginning?
what if this is a beginning,
and i don't acknowledge it?
new, fresh, strange.
not yet mine.

so,
i allowed myself to acknowledge you.
just in case,
i embraced this beginning.
painted a picture to look back at in our old age.
just in case.

what a special moment,
to be lost so close to home.

MERMAID

you built an ocean
in the galaxy
and we swam
in the universe
the sun and moon
in each of us

CONFIDENCE

i wasn't humble,
i just hated myself.

READY

i need a pillow to scream in
a drink to drown in
a wall to throw my fist into

'cause even though
you're long gone
i'm just not prepared to miss you

i wonder
what makes God
laugh?

MIRROR

i saw the way

you saw me

and i loved

what we saw

INFERNO

why do we concern ourselves
    with the meaning of life and death?
don't you know that dying is
    trading one hell for the next?

IRONIC

i obsess so much
over the meaning of life
i swear it's gonna
kill me

QUARANTINE

i don't know where to put my anger.
i exercise.
    a lot.
i create.
    a lot.
i'm with friends.
    a lot.
i work.
    a lot.
i write it down.
    a lot.
i vent.
    a lot.
i do everything i'm supposed to.
    i think.

but i have so much anger inside of me
and i don't know where to put it.
i feel the fire in my chest
burning me from the inside out,
threatening me with spontaneous combustion.
    all day.

maybe i need to scream into some pillows.
maybe i need to break some things.
maybe i need to punch some walls.
but i don't think that's who i want to be.
    i hope.

i hold it tight inside,
forcing my body to convert it into sadness,
and i cry.
     a lot.

i don't know what else to do.
i don't want to be angry with you, anymore.
i want to forgive you,
and i think maybe i have,
because i know you're good inside.
     somewhere.

i know you've been filled with anger for a while,
and i know you don't exercise,
and you don't write it down,
and you don't create,
and you don't spend time with friends.
i know you have a lot of misplaced anger, too.
the difference is, i don't place my anger on you,
and i refuse to.

so, for now,
i'll keep my mouth covered
because i don't want to infect anyone else
the way you infected me.

APPS

i'm sorry,

i just can't meet you

right now

i think i just might like you
and you might just like me, too
and it might just be perfect, so

i'm sorry,

i just can't meet you

right now

WEED

my brain is slow
but my heart is fast
so these minutes feel
like forever

SKY

i fell in
love with

the man on the
moon

because his
distance

reminds me of
you

SWORD

if you want me,
if you miss me,
no matter what you've done to my heart,
i'll expose my chest to you once again.
burn me once, shame on you.
burn me twice, shame on you.
burn me three times,
i'll let you scatter my ashes across the wasteland of your
    selfishness.
i've tried to build armor in callousness
to shield me from the relentless carelessness
of the renters of my heart,
but i've surrendered to the fact that
i always have been and always will be
    this person.
i'll always help people who don't deserve it,
care for people who won't return it,
and fight for people who easily forget it.
i swim oceans for people
who won't cross a teardrop for me,
and if i drown,
    so be it.

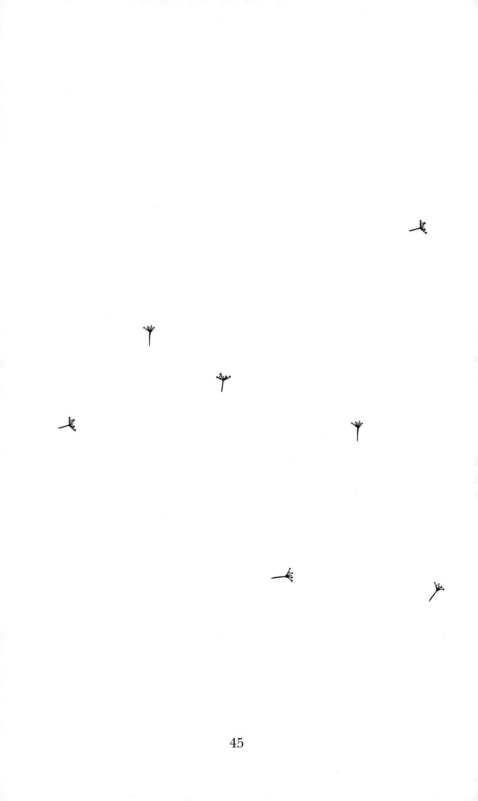

CHECKMATE

i'd have bought you a chessboard
for christmas

yours was missing
some pieces

but you a ways wanted to play

i'd have your last name
engraved in
the side of
the case and

played with you all christmas day

i'd have tried
my best
to master
chess

'cause it'd be nice to share your time

i'd have tried
my best
to master
chess

'cause it'd be nice to win sometimes

i'd have learned
how to move
based on what
you would do

and know to think ahead

i'd have learned
that the Queen
needs the most
protecting

and to kill off a knight instead

more pieces
would get lost
you'd get bored
and you'd toss

it away, that's how you'd repay me

i'd have bought you a chessboard
for christmas
and told you
"this gift is

the best thing you ever gave me."

YAWN

i went to bed at 9 pm
because i felt it was an acceptable
time to say the day was over.

i can justify 9 pm.

that's how my days are, sometimes—
just waiting to go to sleep
so i can say i got through the day.

i've been just-get-through-the-day-ing
so often that i'm terrified
i'll wake up soon
and i'll have gotten-through-my-entire-life.

i usually wake up around 3 or 4,
my heart racing,
choking for breath.

sometimes: nightmares.
usually: bloody.
mostly: an endless loop of
chasing and being chased,
trying to close and lock the door

as some faceless beast pushes back
at me from the other side.

other times: nothing at all.
my nerves are just firing,
sending static through my veins,
keeping me alert for when disaster strikes.

this is what my life has come to.

too depressed to be awake.
too anxious to sleep.

i'm tired.

GRACE

sometimes, at dinnertime,
i open the blinds

    it's fine i can't find
    your eyes in the night

you can see mine
as i'm eating inside

    you can see mine
    'cause i turned on the light

MIDDLE

too old to be relatable

too young to be wise

too smart to be believable

too dumb to be disguised

too dull to be an artist

too creative for nine-to-five

too weak to find my purpose

too strong to say goodbye

HERMIT

i don't want to be bothered
with annoying someone
today

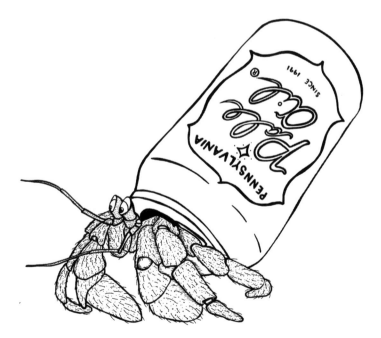

GYM

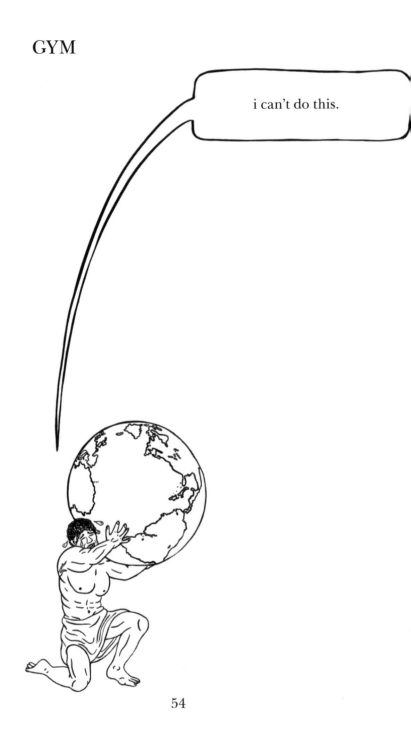

is the weight too much?

WOOF

it's the leash tethered to your spine
right between your shoulder blades
yanking you backward if you dare to push ahead

welded to the vertebrae
making its presence known
whether you pull away or not

you move when master moves
you run when master runs
you stay where master stays

maybe the chain will break
maybe you'll pull hard enough
or maybe, if you're lucky,
master will let you go

you move when you want to move
you run when you want to run
you'd stay if you had a reason

but there's nowhere to go
the unhinged clasp aches
freedom is not a home

you come back to master
some call this loyalty
others call it desperation

good boy

DOGS

running in circles
who's chasing who

SURE

sometimes

    i think
    i've lost
    my mind,

but other times,

    i'm certain

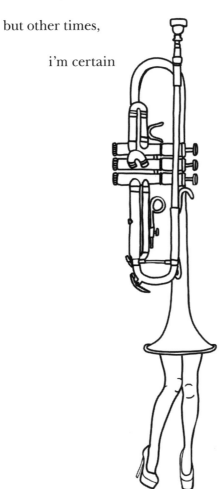

CIVIL

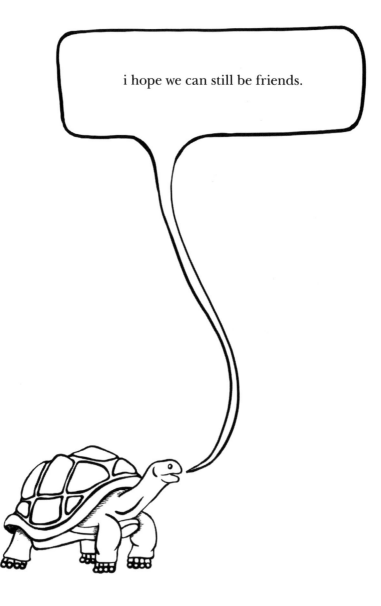

FORGET

all my happiest memories are
with people
who hurt too much to remember

WHISPER

i was sleeping the first time you told me you loved me—
praying i wouldn't hear you,
hoping that i would

i wasn't sleeping the first time you told me you loved me—
pretending i didn't hear you
as hard as i could

DECAF

i put day-old coffee
in a plastic travel cup
because i can't ask the world
for a latte today

FEEL

i used to be ashamed of sensitivity
embarrassed by vulnerability
angry with my empathy

i cry too much
i share too much
i care even for my enemy

i pretended to be hard
tried be strong
attempted to build walls

but then i learned
my bleeding heart
was my greatest gift of all

ONE

sometimes
finding the
right person
just means
realizing
all the things
you thought
mattered
to you

don't

NARCISSIST

don't be fooled when
he stares deeply into your eyes
he's only looking for
his own reflection

LUNCH

we sat together
and ate our pizza
as if everything was okay

we watched together
as a bird hopped along
with a beetle as its prey

we stared together
as the violent bird
ripped the beetle to shreds,

his ferocious beak
tearing away
at the beetle's oozing head

we gawked together
as the beetle tried
to free herself from his beak

a fight to be free
the outcome bleak—
   i was grateful for the company

i wondered if the beetle
understood
the permanence of dying

i was horrified
you were fascinated—
both of us fell silent

the empty shell
of the beetle fell—
the bird hopped away, unfazed

we sat together
and ate our pizza
as if everything was okay

it's okay
if you don't change the world.
it's okay
if you only change one person.
it's okay
if that person is you.

LOVE

just four little letters describe all of you
from your nose to your toes in your tattered ol' shoe.
i know what you're thinking: "that is absurd
to put such big meaning on one little word!"
but that's all it takes! just four tiny symbols
to express how i feel . . . it's really that simple!
that's all i need, just four itty letters—
i promise you no longer word could do better.
write a whole sentence! a paragraph! a novel!
my four-letter word is much more colossal.
it traces your every hair, skin, and blood cell—
just four teensy letters are you in a nutshell.
this puny word is you as a whole;
it embodies your mind, body, and soul!
it describes you in a such a way, i proclaim
that you sign these four letters in place of your name.
you've probably guessed this word, i'd bet;
but if you haven't figured it out just yet,
i'll spell it out for the whole world to read!
these four little letters are C - U - N - T.

WELCOME

every time the doorbell rings
i secretly hope that it's you.

forcing me to listen.
refusing to be ignored.

yesterday, a package delivery.
today, the pool guy.
tomorrow, you, i hope.

WELCOME

every time the doorbell rings
i secretly hope that it's you.

forcing me to listen.
refusing to be ignored.

yesterday, a package delivery.
today, the pool guy.
tomorrow, you, i hope.

ENDLESS

thank you
for the
thank you
card

STORYTIME

the only way it could be worse
is if you didn't tell it.

PLENTY

i really don't get it. you see, i'm a catch,

and you're the shit people reel in and throw back.

i'm strong and i'm mighty and have lots of meat;

you're measly and useless and boring and weak.

i reckon a challenge when i spot a worm,

but you see the hook and then cowardly squirm.

i'm not easy prey and i put up a fight;

you see your predator then swim off in fright.

so why is it, then, that i felt so lucky

to be with a pleb who's less than a guppy?

but you, you don't understand the great fortune

of finding treasure of such disproportion?

i blamed myself once; i questioned my vastness,

doubted my glory and queried my fastness.

but then, i ascertained, it wasn't my fault—

it's just that a minnow can't swallow a shark.

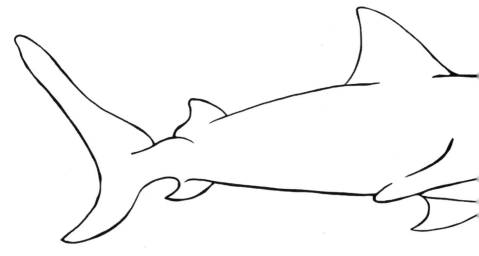

SUPERMAN

they say in
the event of
a shark attack
you're supposed to
punch a shark
square in the nose
which means
at some point
someone figured that out
by punching a shark
square in the nose

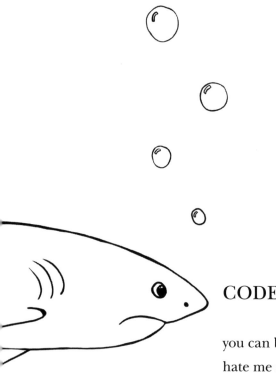

CODEPENDENT

you can bruise me, beat me,
hate me and cheat me,
but i'll still want you forever.

i'll beg you to love me
as you beg to leave me,
and for that, i blame my mother.

SURF

why are we
so drawn to the ocean
as if we have to stand
on the edge of
the world?

VOICEMAIL

i hope i never have to hear
your stupid fucking voice again
but please fucking call me

MISOPHONIA

ha, baby, you're so cute
when you do that thing
where you take such a big bite of food
that your jaw pops when you try to chew
and by chew i mean chomp your food so loud
that it sounds like two horses making out
with mouths full of spaghetti and maggots
it's so adorable that
i want to remove every single one of your teeth
and put them into a blender
until they're just a fine white powder
that i can mix with almond milk
and make you suck down silently
through a straw
and ingest it without making that
super endearing
painfully precious
mind-numbingly lovable
sloshing sound

PITT

they told me
i'd never use my education
but thanks to professor brownell
i know the reason my eyes water
at the sound of my car door unlocking
is i've cried in my car
so many times that
my toyota corolla has become a
conditioned stimulus
which invokes the
conditioned response
of me wanting to die
every time i hear
that stupid fucking beep
just like the dogs
who salivate
at the sound of a bell
and i acquired all this knowledge
at the low cost
of around $136,000

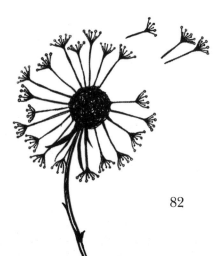

SWEETHEART

fifteen to eighteen
or somewhere between
is the only love i ever felt

but i was young and erratic
and i'm overdramatic
so i'm not sure i trust myself

DROWNING

valentine's day
you're an ocean away
i'll swim it if i have to

i'll do what you say
whatever it takes
as long as i can have you

INDECISIVE

i never want to see you again, for now.

PLAGIARISM

you can't take credit for my sadness,
i earned this on my own.

VILLAIN

am i living in a fabrication of pride and insecurity,
a matrix that exists solely in my mind?
or maybe i've been so badly damaged
that i have no perception of right and wrong.
do bad people know they're bad,
or do they just have a skewed moral compass?
it's hard to imagine anyone waking up in the morning
with the goal of hurting others.
maybe my idea of what's right is wrong.
maybe evil people don't know they're evil,
and they're just doing what they think is right.

      am i a monster or martyr?
      misunderstood or delusional?

the difference between murder and manslaughter is intent,
but either way, someone is dead.

i hope God sees what humans can't.
i hope He can hear the desperation in each heartbeat, the
    loneliness in each breath,
the fear in every explosion, the pain in every fire.
i hope when He examines the crystal ball in my chest He
    sees more Love than Debris.

USELESS

it's a

delightfully devastating
            heart-wrenchingly hopeful
gleefully grim
            terrifyingly tranquil
excitingly excruciating
            painfully pleasant

thing to
not need
you anymore

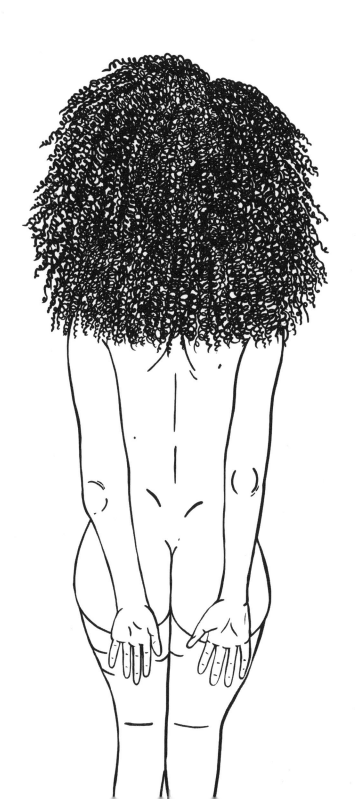

PERHAPS

today is the day i let go of maybe
no fantasies
or daydreams
of what may be

today is the day i let go of maybe
'cause last night
was the last night
you let go of me

COMMITMENT

i don't want a boyfriend
i just want a guy to hang
and grab food with almost every day
and cuddle with every night
who i can introduce to my parents
and also doesn't talk to other girls in any romantic capacity
and maybe in the future if it's something we both
      mutually decide is financially and personally right for us
buy a home
and start a family
nothing serious
i'm chill like that

UNGRATEFUL

you complain about
sand in your house
but you live at
the fucking beach

HOT

where there's smoke
there's fire
or possibly a vape pen
either way
get the hell out of there

ROLLERSKATES

oh my, oh my!
my lace untied!
with graceful glide,
i could have died!
i rolled in stride
not knowing my
skate planned my
untimely demise!

STRAW

your

tears

are

what

broke

me

FRENEMY

being my worst enemy.

EXPLOSION

falling in love with you
was a slow burn to a gas tank

the fire you ignited
was surely worth the wait

leaving you, my love,
was like setting a broken bone

it hurt like hell, but at least
it'll all be better soon

a world without you, my dear,
is like a burger without condiments

a touch more boring, maybe—
but i haven't been hungry since

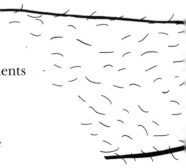

103

DANDELION

when i was a little girl my mama said to me,
      what's your favorite flower, darling? i'll get you the seed.

i said, dandelion! dandelion! that one's so pretty!
      she said, child, that one's not a flower; that one's just a weed.

i still loved those mellow yellow petals anyway.
      what's that thing they say about a rose by any other name?

then my fragile flower turned into a ball of gray,
      so i took a breath and made a wish and blew them all away.

MOURNING

i fucking hate nights like this.

nights after long, productive, exciting days.
a day of distraction
and people
and art
and exercise
and fresh air
and sunshine
and food to eat
and maybe even

happiness.

the type of day that makes you eager to see what tomorrow brings.
the type of day that makes you so hopeful for the future that it
    scares you to your core.
the type of day that makes you thank God that you're alive.

but then the day is over,
and the streets are quiet,
and your mind is screaming.

the people are gone,
and the house feels bigger,
and you feel smaller.

much smaller.

they left you alone here with you,
knowing how you treat you when no one's looking.

pacing from room to room,
searching for
something,
someone,
keeping your body busy
so your mind can rest.

racing from gloom to doom,
yearning for
something,
someone,
anyone to blame
but yourself, for once.

i fucking hate nights like this.

i'll be better in the

morning.

don't be hurt by
people who want to hurt you.
people who want to hurt you
aren't worth hurting for.

TEXT

i blocked your number
so i could stop waiting
on a message . . .

. . . that would never
come

9.13.19

friday the 13th
& a harvest moon
a night built for us
has gone too soon
a starless sky
i still wish for your face
a night built for us
has gone to waste

BULLET

i like making lists.
i always have.
the regular kind, of course.
the to-do lists, the shopping lists.
but i make lists for everything!
i make lists of:

- reasons i'm happy.
- things i'm grateful for
- goals
- nightmares
- things i'd like to try
- things i'm afraid of
- happy memories
and, of course,
- sad memories

sometimes, when the clanging in my head gets just a little
too loud, i take my thoughts out of my brain and put
them on paper. that way, i can leave them at home on my
nightstand while i go about my day. i don't forget them, i
don't lose them, i just put them away for safekeeping. then, i
can revisit the clutter in my storage unit of grief if and when
i need to.
when i let go of someone who was special to me, i make a list.
i make a list of:

- all the ways they mistreated me
- all the nasty things they said to me
- all the times they lied to me

110

- all the ways they hurt me
- all the ways they made me cry
- all the time they made me feel like i wasn't good enough
- all the names they called me

and, of course,

- all the things that love isn't enough to forgive

one time, a boyfriend found a list i wrote about an ex.

he wasn't snooping around or anything,

he was helping me out with something and he just found it.

he was really put off by it.

i told him that sometimes i need to remind myself of why
    not to go back.

he made a comment about how he'd never make a list of all
    the bad things his exes did,

and then we dropped it.

months later, in one of the last conversations we ever had,
    he said:

"write a list about all the things i'm bad at or how shitty of a
    person i am like your ex-boyfriends."

it was one of those things we never talked about.

well, there were plenty of things we never talked about.

but it was one of those things we never talked about that
    was thrown in my face later.

something he held onto for the right moment to unleash it.

a grenade of resentment that was only to be deployed in
    case of an emergency.

a tiny bomb of animosity that could have been defused with
    a little communication.

it was quickly retracted, but i was already covered in shrapnel.

my words and vulnerability were weaponized.

the assumption was that i make those lists to villainize the
    people i once loved,
that i can only see and remember the bad parts about
    somebody—
but it's so very much the opposite.
i make my lists because i was cursed at birth
to see only the good in people.
i forgive over and over and over until i'm left in pieces.
i go back to someone i love for eternity if i allow myself,
because the beatings feel worth the blessings.
but i can't allow myself to do that anymore.
i can't continue the cycle i was raised in,
and i have to remember all parts,
not just the good parts.

so, i make a list. every time i feel weak, drunk on all the
happy memories, i take my thoughts off my nightstand and
put them back in my brain to sober me up.

i don't make lists out of hate.

i don't make lists out of anger.

i make lists because i'll love you forever, but love isn't
enough. i deserve to be treated with respect, and i can't
allow myself to be torn apart anymore.

occasionally, i need a reminder because my heart has a
better memory than my head.

i hold on to all the good parts, too. i just don't need a list to
remember those.

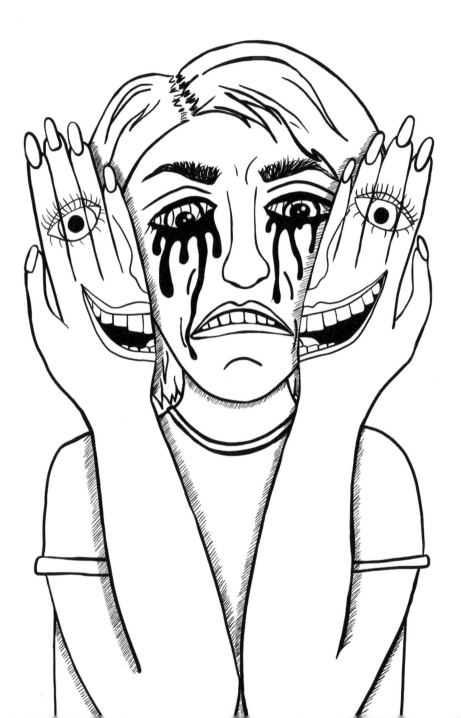

SPLIT

i'm torn between wanting to be open with my history,
and wanting my secrets to die with me.

between allowing someone to allow me to cry,
and not wanting to annoy with negativity.

between living authentically and transparently,
and longing so desperately for privacy.

between praying for happiness and tranquility,
and fearing i'll find it eventually.

NEGOTIATION

what if meeting in the MID

DLE is holding us both back?

if a visitor stops visiting, what are they, exactly?

PITTSBURGH

we could cross that bridge when we get to it,
but i'll most likely burn it first.

dear diary,

sorry to bother
you again.

DISOBEDIENCE

i would have loved you
    as long as you let me
i'll continue to love you
    without your permission

WORDS

"when i love someone, i love them forever."
both of us said it.
neither of us meant it.

BLAME

we can point the finger
at each other
searching for the cause

> but it wasn't my fault
> and it wasn't yours;
> it was both of ours.

cast every stone
we've ever owned
until they turn to dust,

> but it wasn't me
> and it wasn't you;
> they belonged to both of us.

MUCH

build me
up from
dust and
ash

i could never not love you,
so

i'll do
the one
thing you
ask

i love you enough to let you
go

IRONIC

i never felt more
lonely

than when i had the most friends

like

rejection

REDUNDANT

"i think i might be lonely,"
she whispered to herself.

REAL

show me some humility
a little vulnerability
an actual apology
could be nice

take some accountability
communication is a necessity
an ounce of authenticity
would suffice

i'm bored with all the pleasantries
please fuck off with the niceties
before you try to blame me, please
think twice

sometimes you need to lose your mind to find your soul.

COMMUNITY

we all are.

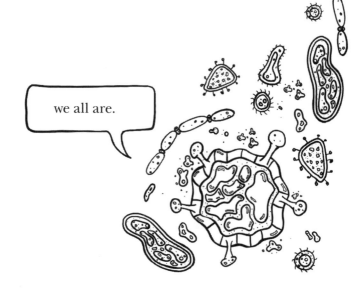

FISHBOWL

i keep every business card someone hands me
as a reminder of all the people i'll never remember

PROSTITUTE

my therapist reminds me
a lot of my ex.

he makes me cry at least once a week
but i keep going back to him.

NARCISSISM

i don't want therapy.

i don't want an hour to focus on myself,
    my shortcomings.
sixty minutes of self-absorption.
three thousand and six hundred seconds of dwelling.

of remembering.
of facing the avoided thoughts.

i don't want this to be the first time
i say this out loud.

in this room,
filled with fake plants and cheap pillows
meant to make it feel "homey,"

    or maybe to lessen the echo in my head.

in this room,
a sounding board for what i want to forget.

in this room,
a reminder that no one's heard it, before.
a reminder that no one's asked, before.

i don't want to pay someone to listen to the shit
no one wants to listen to for free.

maybe my problem is i talk about my problems too much.
maybe my problem is i think my problems
are worth three hundred dollars per hour.

i don't want therapy.

i don't want an hour to focus on myself.
a sixty-minute tug-of-war with my secrets.
a three-thousand-and-six-hundred-second prison.

i want to escape this room.
i want to escape me.

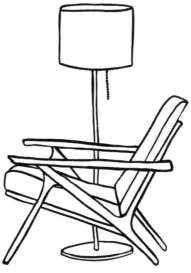

SPACE

you were
never mine
so
never mind,
love

STALKER

i tried to follow my dreams
but they got a restraining order

HANGOVER

the best time
in vegas isn't
the casinos
or the strip clubs
or the shows
it's watching the people at
the casinos
and the strip clubs
and the shows
desperately trying to convince
each other and themselves
that they're having
the best time

BLIND

for Molly

what a cursed blessing
to be forced into guessing
the contents of a heart
without the costume of pride

a beast or a beauty
all comes down, truly,
to not what can be seen,
but what festers inside

no shallow perception
means no misconception—
you can't be distracted
by the vanity dance

it makes me wonder
who'd choose this power
of the shield from deception
if given the chance

DESIRABLE

i've never been
the one that got away
but i *have* been
the one someone escaped from
a time or two

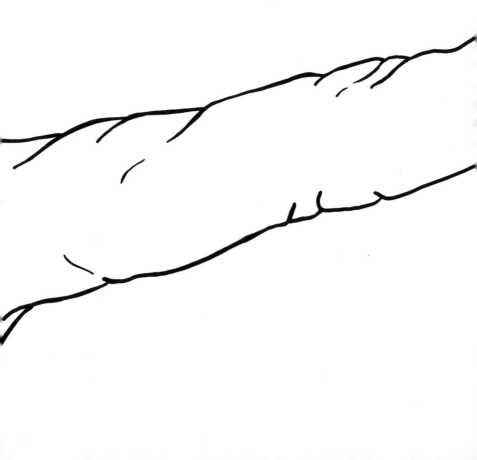

ACT

i'm really not.

ASSAULT

i never told anyone
because i accepted a fifth glass of wine

i never told anyone
because maybe i was a little too flirtatious
at dinner

i never told anyone
because i let him into my apartment

i never told anyone
because maybe i could have been a little louder
with my "stop," a little firmer with my "no"

i never told anyone
because i didn't have any bruises

i never told anyone
because i didn't hit him, i didn't try to push him off,
because i froze when my words weren't powerful enough,
because he was stronger than me and i felt that in his weight

i never told anyone
because no one wants to hear the story
of the girl who made bad choices
and didn't fight back

thank you for letting me tell you

FREDDIE

we don't

sing

but i'll get on

the mic

STANDARDS

you loved how straightforward i am,
as long as i wasn't with you.
  you adored it when i spoke my mind,
  if i didn't talk back to you.

you were turned on by my aggression
as long as i fulfilled all your demands.
  my independence was your obsession
  if i followed your command.

you were desperate for my affection,
but only gave it on your time.
  you're a rusty penny
  who's entitled to a dime.

you're searching for the perfect girl
and i really hope you find her—
  but i have a hunch that if you do
  you won't be what she's after.

RAMBLE

you are a person. a living human organism.

everyone you meet is also a person. a living human organism.

when you are looking at a person, a living human organism,
they are also looking at you, a person, a living human organism.

and as you look at each other, people, living human organisms,
you are experiencing two totally unique, alternate moments
    in the same waking moment.

you are kissing her, but she is kissing you.

you are in a stranger's car, but you are a stranger in someone's car.

you bump into someone, but someone was bumped into by you.

you are heartbroken, but he broke your heart.

people get to know you in a way you never get to know yourself,
because you can't meet yourself.

you don't get to make a first impression on yourself.

you don't get to know yourself better.

you are merely the sum of the perceptions of friends, lovers,
    strangers,

customer service workers.

to one person, you're the moody-looking guy at table three
    who tips pretty well.

to another, you're the asshole who ghosted on tinder.

to another, you're the best friend in the world.

to another, you're your boyfriend's ex, a slutty bitch.

sometimes you're just the pretty girl at the grocery store checkout.

152

once, you were the person who ruined a telemarketer's day by
taking out your anger on them.
maybe twice.
one time you almost hit a cyclist with your car, but that person
is the cyclist who was almost killed.

you're none of those things, and all of those things, and you
never get to pick, and you never get to know.

you are an infinite number of impressions all at once.

you are just a story. you are stories.

live happily ever after.

LIAR

when they ask me if i loved you,
i always tell them no.
it's not that i'm
too embarrassed or
too broken or
too proud to say yes.
it just doesn't feel right
admitting something to them
that i never even admitted
to you.

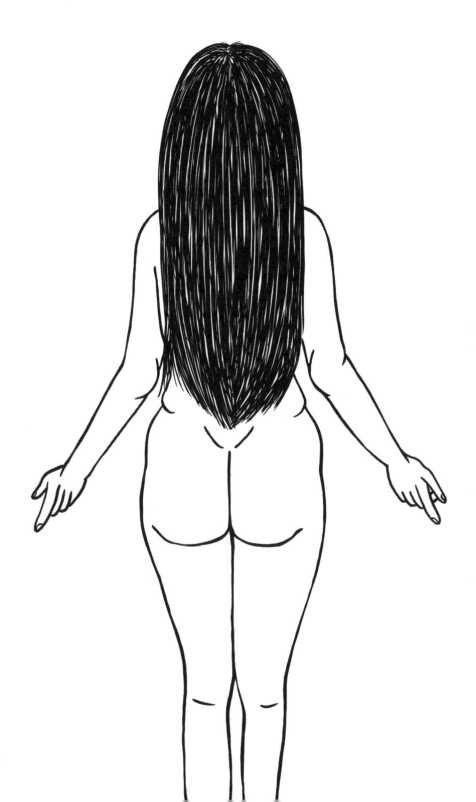

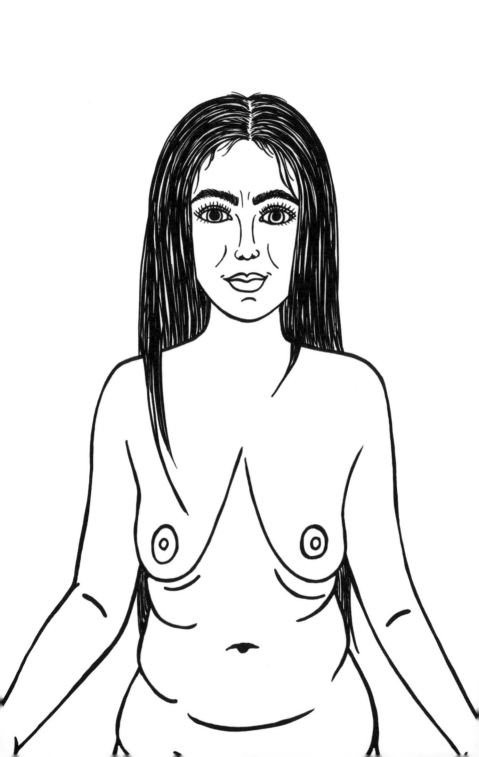

FIGHT

are you moving on, or just giving up?
maybe they feel similar enough.
you can lie to yourself to make it through—
but either way, i'm proud of you.

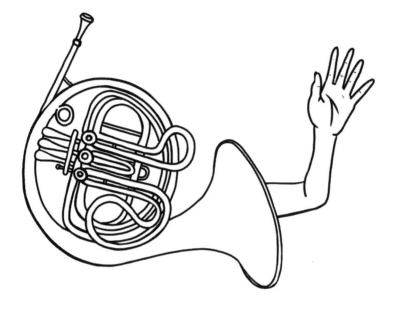

BLOCKED

i can't say hi
   'cause i can't survive
another round
   of drive-by goodbyes

TIMELESS

our hearts don't abide
by the laws of time

at what age am i
frozen inside your mind?

CANDLE

i tricked myself into thinking
you left the darkness behind
but it was dark before you got here
it swallowed you whole while you stayed
and it just remains now that you're gone

DATE

i'm really easygoing
until i'm done pretending
that i'm really easygoing

ANA

she wanted to be a skeleton
one innocent halloween
so she painted up her face
and got a pillowcase of candy

she wanted to be a skeleton
it didn't take long to realize
that the candy in her sack
would go straight down to her thighs

she wanted to be a skeleton
so the boys would think she's sexy
she just wanted to feel loved
for the trade of feeling hungry

she wanted to be a skeleton
so the girls wouldn't tease her
she threw out all her candy
and tried her best to disappear

she wanted to be a skeleton
and so she got her wish
now she's a pretty bag of bones
in a six-foot ditch

if you're ever wondering
how somebody is feeling
but don't trust them
to be honest with you,
just ask them what their favorite
song is at the moment.

HAIRCUT

i wear my hair
short and blonde
because you loved it
long and brown

1.1.20

late afternoon, your head on my lap
"let's watch a movie" means "let's take a nap"
a short-lived attempt 'til your willpower wanes
the tv plays, but i'm watching your face

no thriller could thrill me the way that you do
no horror could scare me like losing you
no comedy could make me laugh like your jokes
no romcom could fill my heart up with hope
like the rise and the fall of your chest as you dream—
we're my favorite movie, it seems

i hope i don't wake you as i play with your beard
you tell me it's fine with a snore in my ear
the diamond on my neck that you put there
thank you, my love, for the happy new year

MORTAL

you're human.

RIDES

i've never understood suicide,
but i understood it today.
until now, it was incomprehensible.
how can life get better if you're dead?
what can be so bad that the alternative is eternal nothing?
don't get me wrong, i've fantasized about dying just like
	everyone else,
but i hadn't considered doing it myself.
never in a million years could i imagine it.
but today, today i was like, "oh."
i'm sad today.
well, i'm sad most days.
but i'm sad today, as well.
someone said to me,
it'll get better. it always does!
and i thought, well, yeah.
and then,
it'll get worse, it always does!
i mean, things couldn't keep getting better
if they didn't keep getting worse.
so, basically, what you're saying is,
things will get better,
because they got worse at some point!
but they will get better again,
and i know this because things got worse!
and this is true.
life will always be an up and down,
a merry-go-round,
of good then bad then better then worse.

but what if your worst is worse than your better?
what if your best isn't better than your worst?
what if you fall much farther than you flew?
if you try to climb out, but you get buried first?

so, i never understood suicide,
but i understood it today.
i understood the hopelessness,
the exhaustion,
the nausea from all the jerky turbulence
and jerky breaths.
i understood that telling someone it always gets better
is just a reminder of how bad it's been
and how bad it can get again.
but please, for the love of God
or whatever it is you do or don't believe in,
please don't.
please live.
please.

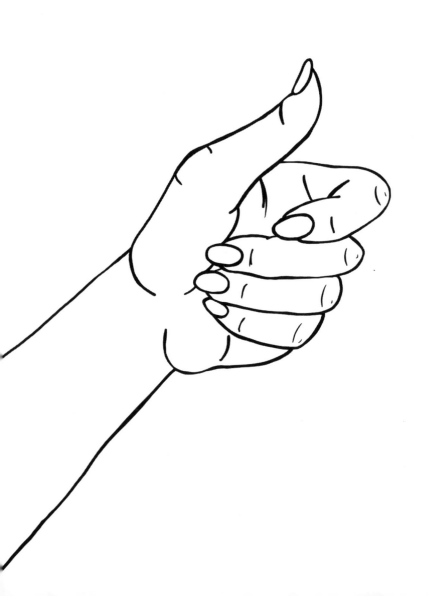

COIN

i want you to know
how much
i resent you
but i can't tell you
how much i hate you
without revealing
how much i loved you

USERS

i do cool things for people
so that they'll
like me
then worry that they only
like me
because
i do cool things for them

175

PROXIMITY

i'm looking for reasons
to hate you.

i have some for ya.

CLOSURE

i miss the feeling
of missing you
but i'll probably stop missing
me missing you, too

GEMINI

the best thing that's happened,
bad for your health,
an angel from heaven,

     all in one breath.

you tell me you hate me
but trap me here with you
'cause you love me so deeply

     until my death.

the perfect woman
a dumb fucking bitch—
who am i today?

     i hate to ask,

but i look in your eyes
and i can't figure out—
which face is you,

     and which is the mask?

AMEN

i used to pray that He would bring you back
but i learned to pray for Him to push me forward

PRAY

if you swear to God
you love me,
so help me God
i'll make you hate me

DECLINE

i lost my credit card
and the customer service woman
asked me for my credit card number
but i don't know my credit card number
because i lost my credit card

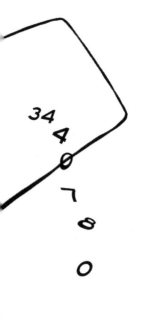

WALK

your advice
was to run
from the cops
but i still
trusted you
with my
freedom

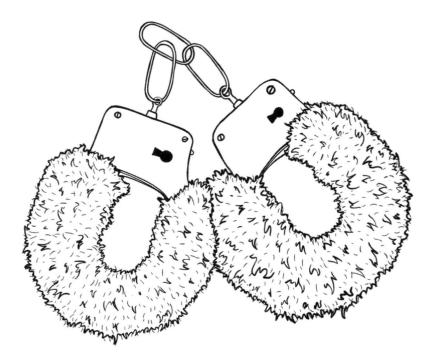

SEVER

i'm jealous of people who can
       cut someone out of their lives
       swiftly sever ties
       drift without a guise

i'm envious of those who
       are graceful with goodbyes
       can quickly abscise
       and easily ostracize

i've never been the type to
       give up so fast
       let you slip from my grasp
       let the past be the past

i hope that someday
       maybe i'll learn
       to let memories burn
       past the point of no return

SOUL

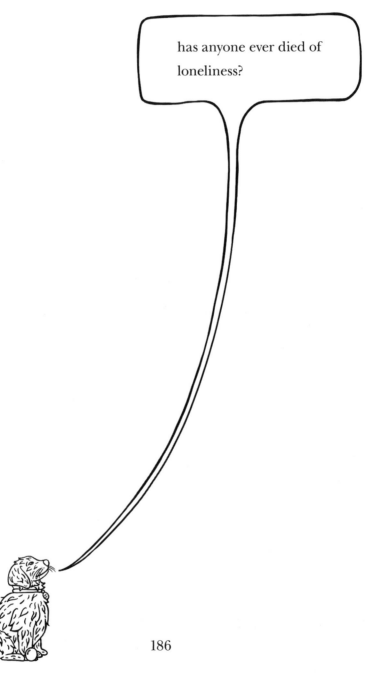

has anyone ever died of loneliness?

FREE

you were my favorite hobby;
such a lovely way to pass the time

VOWS

they broke everything
in the house

'til they had
nothing left to break

but
each other

PLEASANTRIES

"take care,"
he said,

as if he ever cared
about me

CHRISTMAS

i'd give you the world
and you'd still remain silent.
you'd give me your heart
if you knew where to find it.

ROULETTE

there was a time i was afraid of flying
[read: there was a time i was afraid of dying]
      i had way too much to lose,
      i had so much still to live for.

at takeoff and at landing
each violent shaking in between
      my hands searched for each other,
      i'd say a quick, desperate prayer.

but now, thirty thousand miles up
i wonder if maybe i've had enough
      the plummet feels less scary,
      it could be a favor, maybe.

the wheels just safely touched the ground
sighs of relief let out all around
      i, too, let out a breath—
      better luck next time, i guess.

ZZZ

have you ever been
so exhausted
that death seems like
a power nap

RECOGNIZE

a dream where someone you know is in it,
but it doesn't look like them,
yet you know it's them
because of the way
they make you feel

our emotions are smarter than we give them credit for

a moment is
a measurable
amount of time.

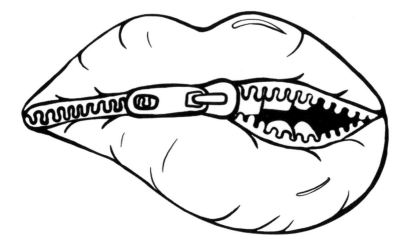

GOSSIP

i don't kiss and tell
'cause even if i had
someone to kiss
i'd have no one to tell

JEALOUSY

i wonder if you wonder
who doesn't have to wonder
what it's like to be with me

SHHHHHHH

'bout what?

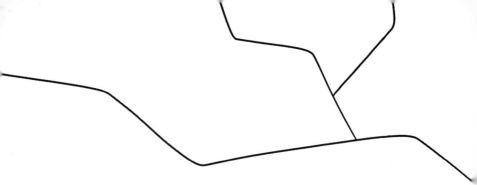

REBOUND

i wish i never knew her name.
i wish i never saw her face.
above it all,
i wish you didn't do it in the first place.
i wish i was enough.
i wish she wasn't so pretty.
above it all, i suppose,
i wish you weren't so quick to replace me.

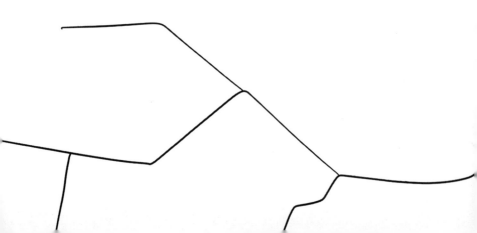

OTHER

a harlot, a vixen
the reason you sin
a whore, a siren
a body to binge
an unknowing homewrecker—
how could you not tell me?
you'll always regret me;
she'll never forget me

HOLIDAY

met you at halloween

liked you by thanksgiving

loved you by christmas

missed you by new year's

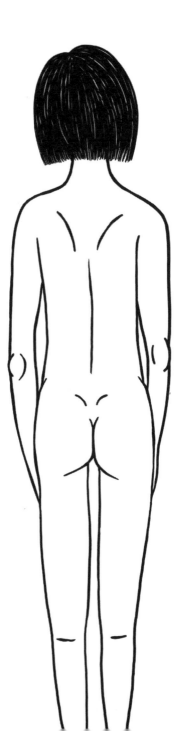

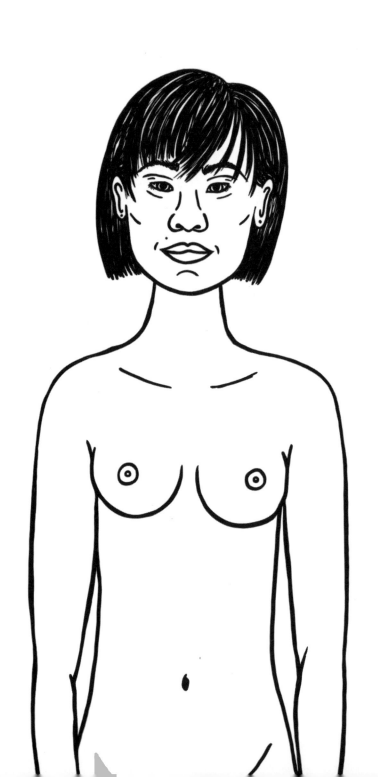

LOVED

how does it feel to be properly
loved,

unconditionally
loved,

irrevocably
loved?

worth the effort
loved,

one and only best friend
loved,

"i'm so happy you were born"
loved?

    i sure would like to be loved
    like that,
    one day.

    i sure hope i deserve to be loved
    like that,
    one day.

HOPE

someday
somehow
somewhere
someone
might
somewhat
care

207

THIRSTY

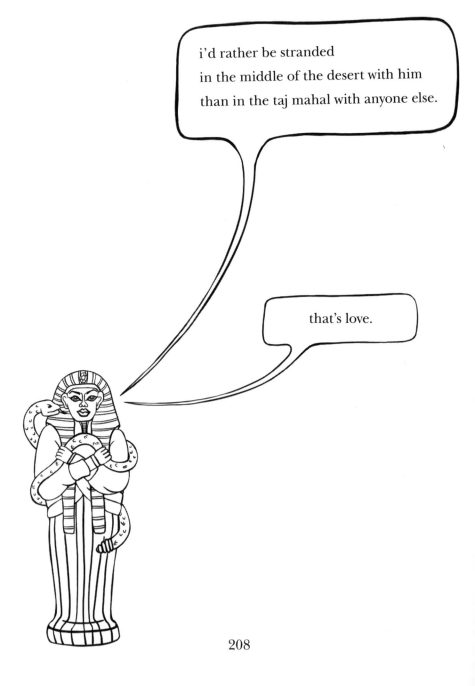

i'd rather be stranded
in the middle of the desert with him
than in the taj mahal with anyone else.

that's love.

PENPAL
34

i often write letters
to the universe because
i don't know your address

KETTLE

they call your misfortune
                    bad karma
they call their misfortune
                    bad luck

POVERTY

i don't buy expensive cars because i'm afraid i'll have
    nowhere to drive.

i live in a shitty apartment because i'm afraid a house
    will feel too empty,
a mortgage too permanent.

what if i have everything i want and i'm still not happy.

then what.

SHOOT

be wary of the price,
be sure of your desires

the fire melts the ice,
but the water kills the fire

KING

i can't wait to get
under the covers
at night so i can think
about you.

remember you.

pray to have you
in the bed i used to share with you.

i think this is what it is to miss you.

i miss you.

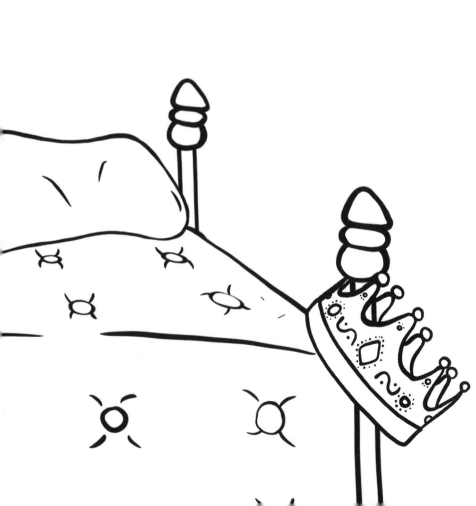

TRAGEDY

i'm too happy.

i survive on melancholy the way a coroner depends on death.
singing songs of sorrow as distraction from disaster,
erecting shrines in honor of the things that destroyed me,
bottling my bad blood and drowning myself with it.
i don't know how to write about anything but pain.
but i have no pain.

i'm too happy.

even in chaos, i'm happy.
my brain feels different.
i've come to the conclusion that everything will, in fact, be okay.
i've survived monsoons and earthquakes and tornadoes in
    my mind,
landslides and avalanches and hurricanes in my heart.
and i deserve this, i deserve to be happy, but—

i'm too happy.

uninspiring happy.
problematic happy.
i'm home, but i'm my best when i'm lost.
i'm safe on shore, but i miss the turbulence.
i'm longing for someone to rock the boat,
but please,

don't.
not yet.

let me feel safe for a while,
but just for a while.
don't let me get too comfortable,
but give me a moment.
give me this vacation—
i've worked long enough.

let me be too happy,

just for a bit.

STORIES I HAVE TO GET
DRUNK TO TELL

Hello

I've been holding on to anger for most of my life. I've always told myself, "Someday, you'll get to tell your story. And when you do, you'll be ready." This was supposed to be that moment, the moment I got to share my secrets, the moment I set everything free. I was convinced I was ready to release what I've carried with me my whole life, to turn my trauma into something valuable. That it would in some way heal me.

Yet, for months I sat in front of my laptop, trying to put my stories on the page, trying to find the words. As the deadline approached, I had to ask myself, "Why? Why are you having so much trouble? What's holding you back?" And then I realized: I don't want to hold on to what hurt me anymore.

I haven't been angry in a very long time, and I don't want to go back. Not right now. I've spent years, most of my life, blaming my parents for the rough start I had. I blamed them for my anger issues, my trust issues, my anxiety and depression. I blamed them for my failed and abusive relationships, for never teaching me how to love and be loved. I blamed them for my toxic relationship with money, with food, for never providing me with a sense of security or safety.

But I turned out okay. I own a beautiful home; I'm in a loving relationship and have darling friends. I spend my days working on things that make me happy, and I've turned that into a living. I can afford whatever I need and have the opportunity to save. And still, I have bad days. Still, I find myself acting in a way that I'm ashamed of.

As an adult with an array of mental health issues, I have to work to keep myself level. I've had a lot of therapy; I need a lot of alone time; I need a lot of quiet. My anxiety, depression, and ADHD make everyday tasks feel monstrous, and I have no one to look after but myself. I look at my life—twenty-nine and comfortable, no real-life stress or children to worry about—and I'm not always the best version of myself. I'm easily agitated, often overwhelmed, and constantly catastrophizing. I compare where I am at twenty-nine with where my parents were at the same age, and the difference is astronomical. At my age, my parents were trapped in a unhealthy marriage with three kids they couldn't afford.

Imagining my parents with the same mental health issues and worse, living under the conditions in which they were living, my resentment changed into empathy. I can't fathom the immense pressure and stress they had to navigate every day, and how I would react in the same situation. A lot has changed in the thirtysomething years since my mom and dad became parents. I've always told myself that if it weren't for my parents I wouldn't be who I am today, and I've always said it in a negative way. But the truth is, all of the most wonderful parts of me come from them, too.

My mom has never for a moment not believed in my dreams. She's fed my hunger for music and performance for as long as I can remember. I watched in awe as she played her flute, or when she was the lead in a play. I used to tell everyone sitting around me in the theater, "That's my mom." Without her pushing me to join the choir, insisting that I play instruments, introducing me to dance at a young age, it's hard to say if I would be in entertainment at all. Any interest I showed in an extracurricular activity, she was there to support it. She not only took me to audition for local theater productions, she volunteered as head of the wardrobe department so she could be involved. It made me feel so important to tell everyone that my mom was in charge of all the costumes.

My mom wrote her own lullabies and sang to us every night, encouraging us to sing with her. Long car rides were made bearable by impromptu sing-alongs and rounds. At any given moment, we would all break out in song and dance. I *still* break out in song and dance—that comes from her. She used to hand-sew all of our Halloween costumes because the store-bought ones weren't unique enough for her girls. If I told her I was thinking about doing something, she told me, "So do it."

My dad is a writer and artist. I used to find beautiful drawings around the house and ask where they came from, and I was shocked to find out he did them. He had journals in which he would write poetry and draw pictures, and sometimes, he would share them with us. He was a brilliant decorator; every corner of my house had a mysterious, whimsical feel to it. My dad would carve intricate relics and scenes out of wood, then meticulously paint them. He collected antiques; he was obsessed with the abnormal, the rare. We were exposed to incredible indie artists and rock bands, beautiful and odd films. Our bedtime stories were from Edgar Allan Poe, the Brothers Grimm, Hans Christian Andersen. He had an affinity for tradition and nostalgia that's become deeply ingrained in my personality.

He bought my first book, *Adultolescence*, knowing I would give him a copy, and had me sign it the moment I got home. He brags about me to his friends and coworkers any chance he gets. When I asked him how he felt about me sharing stories of my childhood, he responded, "You know I'm a fair man when it comes to artistic needs, and I'm sure I will understand anything you need to write about."

It's been hard to remember the good times through all the trauma, but just as nothing is black and white, neither are they. They're complicated. They've also had a life of chaos and fear. They're not perfect, they're not well, but they love. To share the personal, intimate details of my life would be to share the personal, intimate details of *their* lives. Of my siblings' lives. My grandparents' lives. But this isn't just my story to tell. So, for now, I'll keep most of our secrets safe. I hope you can take something from the ones I can share with you now.

Thank you for wanting to be a part of my story.

The Second Hot Dog

I remember the exact moment I started hating my body. It was the catalyst of a lifelong battle with low self-esteem, self-loathing, and an array of eating disorders. Funny, what a second hot dog can do.

My mom was always on a diet when I was growing up. No-carb. No-fat. Tofu with sugar-free chocolate powder. Diet pop. Sweetener packets dumped into plain low-fat yogurt. Late-night bingeing followed by 5 a.m. workout tapes. When it came to us kids, though, our food intake wasn't what I would call regulated, or really even monitored. Granted, the '90s were a very different time when it came to health education and information. It was a time where SunnyD was the equivalent to orange juice, and orange juice was considered a healthy alternative to pop. Sugar wasn't a concern, artificial sweeteners and chemicals were science fiction. Calories were king, nothing else mattered . . . and kids didn't count calories.

Being poor definitely didn't help my relationship with eating. One of the greatest tragedies of the modern world is how accessible nutritionally empty, high-calorie foods are and how unattainable organic, nutrient-rich foods are for most middle-to-lower-class citizens. If you have a family of four to feed, you're not going to grab a cut of quality meat from the butcher and fresh produce to feed them for the night; you're going to buy the case of ramen to feed them for a month. You could splurge and buy some hamburger meat, buns, cheese, and ketchup, but you're more likely going to stop at McDonald's and get a burger for 99 cents instead. Like most of America, I was raised on generic, processed, frozen, and boxed options. Sometimes, we relied on food banks or government assistance. Other times, we relied on the kindness of family and friends. The worst of times, we got food from the trash (until we got caught).

My parents made sure we got to school early enough to eat the free breakfast—some type of dessert or breakfast pizza. We qualified for free lunch, so we didn't waste any money on packing one. The way our lunch was set up, you either paid or you didn't when you reached the end of the line. That means that if you got free lunch, anyone around would know it. The first half of my school career was spent doing everything I could to not be seen. I patiently waited until every other student got their meal, insisting that I wasn't hungry when my classmates

225

asked me if I was getting in line with them. Or, I lingered in the hallway, mindlessly shuffling through papers in hopes of appearing to be busy. When everyone was seated and eating, I would say something along the lines of, "Eh, I guess I'd better eat—I don't want to be hungry later." When the coast was clear, I would slip into the cafeteria and swiftly grab a tray without the prying eyes of my classmates.

It only took one kid, one time, to yell, "Oh my God, you get free lunch?" for me to never allow myself to eat a tray lunch again.

After that, I would use my birthday or Christmas money to buy something à la carte. Greasy, high-carb options like soft pretzels and pepperoni rolls became my staples. Occasionally, if I felt too guilty spending the money, I would get an ice-cream bar for 35 cents. Many times, I pretended to be on a diet; I went hungry until I could get home and binge on whatever junk food was on clearance that week. Every time I would eat, my brain would go back to that moment, to that fucking hot dog.

One of my favorite things in the world as a kid was our backyard campfires. My dad made a little fire pit in the driveway and we would pretend to be camping. We didn't get to spend a lot of quality time together without fighting, so I cherished the rare occasions when my parents made the time for us to sit and eat as a family. Cooking our own dinner over the open flames, we got to do an activity together *and* we got to enjoy a meal together. I just loved everything about it.

On this particular night, when I was around seven years old, we were having hot dogs for dinner with s'mores for dessert. When you're raised without much, it's easy to overindulge when the opportunity presents itself. There's not always food, so you'd better fill up while it's there. There aren't always treats, so you'd better enjoy them while they last. When your norm is splitting one candy apple among five or more people, it's hard to resist seconds when they're available.

I had just finished my first hot dog, and I was excited for a second. I cooked up another one and dug in. About halfway through, I decided I was too full and wanted to save room for a s'more or two. Mouth still full of hot dog and bun, I asked my family seated around the fire, "Does anybody want the rest of this? I'm full."

My mom promptly responded with, "Jesus, Gabrielle. Why do you always have to stuff yourself to the point that you can't eat anymore?"

I stopped chewing. I didn't understand the question. I thought the point was to stop eating when you were full, and I was full, so I stopped eating. I felt everybody's eyes on me, and suddenly I became aware of the way my belly hung slightly over my basketball shorts. Unable and unwilling to swallow, I threw the remainder of my hot dog and ran upstairs, where I spit the soggy mouthful into the toilet. I then retreated to my room, where I slammed the door, opened up a coloring book, and tried to color a picture through the blurriness of my stinging tears.

I keep repeating that phrase in my head: *Why do you always have to stuff yourself to the point that you can't eat anymore? Why do you always have to stuff yourself to the point that you can't eat anymore?* I was looking forward to s'mores all day, excited to have a campfire with my family, and now I was in my room, whisking away the rogue tears that I couldn't hold back.

I'm not sure how much time passed before I heard a knock at the door. I stiffened up and straightened my face, careful not to let anyone know I was crying. In a sweet voice, my mom asked, "Why don't you come back out and make s'mores with us?" Eyes fixated on the page and hand scribbling without direction, I responded, "No." That's all I could manage without my voice cracking, without giving myself away. She quickly retaliated with, "Fine, stay up here and cry—I don't care."

The moment the door slammed behind her, I flung myself onto the floor and sobbed into my pink teddy bear, a gift after a trip to the hospital.

I was too young to understand what I was feeling, but as an adult, I recognize it as shame. That shame followed me for two decades, through every bite of every meal. It turned to anger, it turned to bad habits, it turned to judging others to avoid facing myself. It turned to sneaking extra food when no one was looking, to eating in the dark or with the refrigerator door open. It led to starving myself for days, then bingeing for days, then starving myself again. It led to chewing entire packages of cookies or chips, whole candy bars, and spitting them out. It led to cavities; it led to a broken metabolism. It led to private and public meltdowns over calories or unhealthy food options. It led to years and years of wanting so desperately to be healthy and fighting myself every step of the way.

It took a lifetime of weight fluctuation, years of therapy, and a handful of failed attempts with nutritionists and trainers to get where I am now. Today, I'm proud to say that I have a (mostly) healthy relationship with food. I recognize my body as a tool to help me achieve all the things I want to achieve, not something to be scrutinized. I've turned my attention to being strong, not "skinny." I know my mom didn't mean to hurt me back then; she was young and struggling herself. She deflected her own unhealthy relationship with food onto me, just as I've deflected mine onto others.

To any of you fighting yourself about food, just know that I see you and understand you. I know it feels like you'll never be "normal," that you'll never be able to enjoy food without obsessing over it, but I promise you that there's a light at the other end of this. I never thought I'd see the day that I would be able to eat dessert and not have an anxiety attack over it. Never in a million years did I imagine I would be able to keep chips in my house without chewing and spitting out the entire bag at once, that I would be able to have snacks without fixating on them. When I was seven, I lost sight of the fact that food was meant to be enjoyed and now, I'm able to enjoy it.

You will be healthy again. You owe that to yourself.

The Waiting Game

He was screaming again, but this time felt different. Menacing. I couldn't tell you today what he was so angry about; I didn't even know then. I never knew. By this point, I had stopped trying to guess.

He seemingly hated me but wouldn't let me leave him. He sunk his teeth in, filling me with venom, but would clench harder if I tried to pull away. He ignored my calls if I wanted him near, but he would stalk me when I wanted him gone. He would tell me he was done with me, but then destroy any chance of me forming a new relationship. It was made very clear: I was his property.

He was seething again, but this time felt different. Fatal. I'd never seen his crystal blue eyes so black, his pale skin so red. He was towering over me in nothing but his boxers, his entire body swaying with the intensity of his breathing. His fists were clenched to the point of shaking on either side, elbows bowed and ready to unleash.

My keys, phone, and shoes were taken from me; I was being held hostage. I asked him to please, please let me leave. He told me no. I asked him to please, please let me have my things. He told me no. The door behind him led out to the alleyway that our apartments shared. Recognizing the challenge of trying to get past him, I slowly backed into the open doorway of his bedroom. I tried to remember the exact layout of the apartment behind me, planning my escape through the main entrance.

Just as I was about to sprint barefoot from his apartment, his roommate walked in with whatever girl he had brought home that night. I locked eyes with him, silently pleading for him to stay. With a scoff and a roll of his eyes, he walked back out as suddenly as he'd entered.

My heart dropped as I sucked in a breath, and before I could fully turn back around to face him, he grabbed me by the neck and slammed me against the doorframe. He closed the door on my back and shoulders over and over before squeezing me one last time, trapping me there.

The door released and he pulled me back into the room, locking the exit behind me. I asked him what he wanted.

"Get on your knees and beg."

I did as I was told.

"Tell me how much you don't deserve me."

I did as I was told.

"Suck my cock, fucking bitch."

I asked him if I could please have my things, if we could please have a nice night.

"You're going to try and leave as soon as I give them back."

I reassured him that I would stay. That I loved him and wanted to enjoy the evening together.

As he turned to get my belongings, I subtly positioned myself closer to the other door. The moment he placed them in my hand, I sprinted with everything in me outside, across the alleyway, and into my apartment. My room was in the basement, so no one heard me enter.

No one heard him enter.

How could I fail to deadbolt the door? I crawled into my bed and pulled the covers to my chin, trying to disappear into the darkness. As I saw his silhouette looming in the doorway, still in nothing but his boxers, I told myself, "You're going to die tonight." I held my breath as he slowly, painfully slowly, walked toward me. Every hair on my body stood up as he gingerly pulled the cover from me. Every muscle tensed as he lay down next to me, wrapping his arms around me in a way that reminded me what he could do, if he wanted.

He was whispering, but I could feel him screaming.

"You can't ever leave me," he hissed into my ear.

"I know," I confessed.

"Tell me you'll love me forever," he demanded.

"I'll love you forever," I lied.

He fell asleep. I didn't close my eyes all night.

After that, it was a waiting game. I was alone. He had already told everybody I was crazy, and everybody believed him. Honestly, maybe I was. I don't know how I couldn't be. The same friends who had wiped the blood from my knees when he pushed me down, the same friends who asked me why I was always covered in bruises—they were gone now. I was afraid to go to the police, because everyone would say that I was just trying to ruin his life.

So, I waited. I waited, and I graduated, and then I was free.

An Incredible Disappointment

I've never been someone who gets hit on very often. At the most, I'm the girl you take a pass at when the bar is closing and everyone else is taken. He was the bartender, and a very good-looking one at that, so it came as a welcome surprise when he asked me out on a real date. Dinner. I took inventory of all the other single women, all thinner, all more beautiful than I was. Somehow, for some reason, he chose me—a mere mortal in the City of Angels.

I had never felt better about myself, more confident. I had given up on dating in LA, accepting the fact that I could never compete with the perfect faces and bodies that populate this city. Accepting that I would just have to learn to coexist with the loneliness. But tonight? Tonight, I smiled the whole ride home, telling myself fairy tales of love and hope.

He made a reservation at an expensive restaurant; the

gesture made me uneasy. I wasn't even used to men offering to pay for dinner, let alone go through the effort of making a reservation. I looked up the menu and shuddered at the prices . . . I knew I wasn't worth that. I imagined him getting the bill and being aggravated at the total. I imagined myself insisting that he let me pay at least half, since he'd wasted his evening in my company.

I prepared myself to be an incredible disappointment.

All my worries vanished the moment he arrived to pick me up. He had one of those personalities that just calmed you. God, he was so charming. He smiled at me, told me how happy he was that I had agreed to go out with him. As if there was any universe in which someone like me would turn down someone like him! Maybe there's something wrong with him, I thought to myself. Or, maybe, he doesn't realize how attractive he is. Or, maybe, *just maybe*, I was more worthy than I gave myself credit for.

After a few brief minutes, we arrived at the restaurant. We circled in the car for a while looking for a valet or parking, but on a Saturday night in LA, I knew our chances were slim. Since I lived so close, I made a suggestion:

"We're not far from my place. Why don't we just park in my garage and Uber here? Way easier."

"Are you sure? I don't want to impose," he politely responded.

"Of course! It makes way more sense," I insisted. And with that, we headed back to my place, parked, and Ubered back.

Dinner was amazing. Well, not that place; that place sucked. The clientele was snobby and the service slow, so I suggested we get out of there and go to a different spot down the street. We walked hand in hand all the way down Sunset Boulevard and found ourselves overdressed at my favorite hole-in-the-wall, filling up on fried yucca and wine. And we laughed. Oh, wow, we laughed.

It was the best date I'd ever been on.

Three bottles of wine later, the manager was kicking us out. When I offered to split the bill, he laughed at me and gave the waiter his card. We Ubered back to my place, both of us visibly drunk. It was clear he was in no shape to drive, and I couldn't in good conscience allow him to get behind the wheel for his hour-long journey home.

My mind raced back to college, back to the last time I had allowed myself to be alone in a room with a drunk man I barely knew, and I shivered. I quickly brushed the memory away. He wasn't like that; he wouldn't do that. He was kind. He was charming. I invited him in, but firmly set the boundaries and expectations for the rest of the evening.

"I don't think you should drive. You're welcome to come upstairs, but just until you sober up. I'd rather just take anything physical off the table for tonight, if that's okay?" I anxiously awaited his reply.

"Yeah, of course! No pressure; let's take it slow," he responded as I let out a breath.

Moments later, we were in the elevator.

Moments later, we were on my couch.

Moments later, he was kissing me.

Moments later, he was unhooking my bra.

Moments later, I was asking him to slow down.

Moments later, he was pulling off my pants, my underwear.

Moments later, I told him no.

Moments later, he didn't listen.
Moments later, I told him no.
Moments later, he didn't listen.
Moments later, I told him no.
Moments later, he didn't listen.
Moments later, I told him no.
Moments later, he didn't listen.
Moments later, I quietly asked him to please stop.
Moments later, he asked, "Wait, really?"
I answered him with silence.

Finally, he stopped. He got dressed. He left. Drove drunk the whole way home. I don't remember crying, but I do remember tears rolling down my cheeks for days. How stupid I was to think someone like me could be with someone like him. How silly I was for getting my hopes up that I might be worth something to someone. How foolish I was to let a drunk man into my apartment.

The next day, he texted me and asked if I would go on a second date with him, completely oblivious to what he had done. I never responded.

What an incredible disappointment.

The Pink Journal

My mom was a hoarder.

That's something I hid from for the majority of my life. No one knew, because no one came over. The humiliation haunted me every day when I showed up to school, wondering if anyone could smell the aroma of filth and must wafting from my clothes. It wormed its way into my adulthood as I tried to fight the learned behavior of holding on to items that were no longer needed. The fear of having nothing was ingrained so deeply in my psyche that I learned to keep, well, *everything*.

Growing up was lonely. I couldn't invite people over to my house, so no one invited me over to theirs. I watched longingly as the entire cheerleading squad walked together to one of their homes to hang out after practice, the only one who wasn't invited being me. I listened desperately as the kids at school talked about the movies they'd watched the night before, as they roared with laughter at the inside jokes. I didn't get to laugh. I was on the outside.

My days weren't spent gossiping or swimming with friends. They were spent at home, raising the younger kids and trying to keep up with the mess. My mom demanded that I clean the house, but didn't allow me to throw anything away. It was as if she was hoping I could somehow turn trash into treasure, polish the dumpster in which we were living. Morning to night, screaming to clean. Morning to night, cleaning. Morning to night, screaming that I cleaned the wrong place, the wrong way. Morning to night, staring in hopelessness as the trash bags I filled were ripped apart and thrown back across the floor. It was a battle I could never win.

My nights weren't spent at sleepovers or on the phone with friends. They were spent waking up with the kids when they needed to be fed or changed. They were spent comforting them when they were woken up by the screaming. They were spent trying to stop the fighting between my parents. It was breaking glass, the sound of my childhood home being ripped apart piece by piece. After school, if I tried to take a nap to catch up on lost sleep, I was shaken awake by a thunderous voice demanding that I clean. It was violence. It was shouting. It was being put to work, raising children, chasing after a never-ending mess. It was being punished for doing it all wrong. It was hell.

My dad didn't help. He believed everyone should clean up after themselves. So, he washed his own dish. He did his own laundry. He took care of his own belongings. At some point, I think he forgot that there were four younger children who needed their dishes to be washed. Who needed their laundry to be done. Who needed the bathtub to be cleaned, the floors swept, their rooms dusted. He wanted to be angry about the mess, but he didn't want to do anything about it. This wasn't his responsibility. It was mine and my older sisters'.

One day, I was cleaning the single bathroom shared by nine people. The cabinets were filled with empty bottles, half-used hotel toiletries, expired hair dye that stained the countertop. Junk mail and school projects that made their way upstairs, covered in oil and stains. Old magazines, soaked in water and whatever else you might find in a bathroom, crumpled and curling at the edges. A decade of toothbrushes, always multiplying, never thrown away. Makeup and nail polish that would give you an infection if you dared to use it.

I picked all the laundry up off the floor and put it in the hamper, then took the hamper to the basement to join the mountains of mold-covered clothing. I wiped down the countertop, trying my best to ignore the rust and discoloration that couldn't be removed, grateful we never had guests. I started to fill a black garbage bag with toilet paper rolls, ripped papers, food packages, and other miscellaneous trash that somehow wound up on the bathroom floor. It took some time, but the bathroom looked . . . livable.

My mom came home from who knows where as I was tying the black bag, furious that I'd cleaned the bathroom instead of the kitchen. She demanded that I tell her what was in the bag. Trash, I told her. The trash bag was full of trash.

She yanked the bag from my hands and tore it open like a piñata, splaying all my hard work across the floor. She frantically grabbed at the pile like a child at a birthday party, plucking out miniature bottles and crumpled papers. Her hands found an old, pink, sparkly journal. The spine had been entirely cracked, causing it to limply flop around as she waved it in my face. The sad, unused paper was empty of any writing, but filled with stains and bacteria of every variation. The pages were ripped and folded in a way that prohibited the journal from laying flat, that warned against trusting it with your most personal thoughts.

It was garbage.

She scolded me for being wasteful, for throwing away her things. She berated me for causing more work for her, for wasting her time. She shoved that journal in my face the way my dad pushed our dog's face into her own shit to teach her what she had done wrong.

That was my breaking point. I snatched the disgusting, pink, sparkly journal from her hands, cocked back, and launched it at her face. I did it without thinking; it was primal. As it turns out, being raised with violence makes you violent. In shock at what I had just done, I noticed a small red circle form just above her eyebrow. I stared in panic as a thin stream of blood trickled down her face. Then, I ran.

I was much bigger than her, but I felt small. Scared. She called the police, but when they came to the door, I hid. I think my dad talked to them; I honestly don't know. That wasn't the first time she tried to have me arrested, but it was the first time I actually did something to make me feel like I deserved it.

An hour later, it was like nothing had ever happened. Everything went back to the way it always was. That was usually how it went down—a huge eruption, followed by nothing.

I went to the kitchen and started on the dishes.

Goodbye

I used to meet all my friends online. We would find each other on Myspace or in chatrooms, add each other on AOL Instant Messenger and meet up every night. This was when "video chat" was something people wrote about in sci-fi movies and futuristic films. No, I'm not that old. Technology just moves that fast.

I just wanted companions, to feel like I belonged, like I was accepted. On the rare occasions that the "cool kids" threw me a bone and invited me into their circle, I didn't know how to be around them. Partly because my complete and utter lack of socialization left me clueless on typical teenage behavior; mostly because I couldn't connect in the way I knew I was supposed to with kids my age.

The conversations always felt like an awkward first date.

Forced. Careful not to talk over them or accidentally start a sentence at the same time. Aware of how my face looked, my body language, their body language. Focusing so hard on things that should come naturally but don't that I would stop listening, and then I'd panic that I might not know how to answer next because I wasn't listening.

Since I struggled so much to make real-life connections, I turned to my dial-up internet connection. I spent a lot of time online trying to build popularity on Myspace so I could create the fantasy of a world where people cared about me. And then, people actually started caring. I made friends. Real friends. Chosen by choice, not proximity. People who shared my interests, artistic people, smart people. A beautiful group of interesting, lovely, intelligent, eclectic little weirdos. There for each other for no reason other than we chose to be. Family. People I could tell my deepest secrets to because I had nothing to lose. Behind a screen; transparent but protective.

I built relationships I couldn't muster in real life because it wasn't embarrassing to be on the internet. No one online knew that my dad drank a lot or my mom screamed a lot. It was just me. No one to make my reputation for me. Just me.

My internet friends were all I had. They saved me.

Then one day, people started caring about what I had to say. A lot of people, all at once. And then a lot more people. It was like my dreams came true. The fantasy I lived on Myspace was becoming a reality. People liked me. They were listening.

I'm not sure when exactly, but soon it reached a point where I wasn't allowed to make friends online anymore.

I was no longer just an anonymous misfit on the internet, so the dynamic shifted without my permission. It felt like I was being shamed or punished for speaking to my fans on a personal level. But it never felt like a "public figure" speaking to a "fan." To me, it was a human being connecting to another human being, the way I always had. Somewhere along the line, it got twisted into something inappropriate, maybe even dark.

I pulled back.

Then it became about, who could I trust? Who's here as someone who connected with me, my art, my music? And who's here because they want to "expose" me? If I made a friend online, how would I know they wouldn't share all my secrets if we got in an argument? If I vent, will it be used against me? Did they ever like me in the first place, or was it all an act to get something to hold over my head? For attention?

I pulled back some more.

A lot more.

For a long time, I avoided any type of interaction with anyone because I didn't know who was who, which was which. I was so focused on trying to look away from the internet that I forgot what brought me here in the first place.

One night, I discovered that there was a video chatroom in my Discord server (fine, I'm that old). I hopped in for a minute to say hello. I ended up staying for a bit, longer than I usually feel comfortable. I let myself be more than just an entertainer. I allowed myself to be human, again.

I discovered a whole little underground world, a tucked-away minuscule corner of the internet that exists only for the people who find it. Who search for it. I saw that the people in the server are *friends*. Real, genuine friends. They meet every night and hang out because that's what makes them happy. They get to spend time with the people they care about. People who share their interests, artistic people, smart people. A beautiful group of interesting, lovely, smart, eclectic little weirdos. There for each other for no reason other than they chose to be. Family. People who they can tell their deepest secrets to, because they have nothing to lose. Behind a screen; transparent but protective.

I got to experience something very rare and special that made my heart ache in a good way. Usually when I get to meet people, especially in groups, there's a few minutes of excitement and compliments before the interaction ends. The people closest to me know I'm not comfortable being the center of attention in real life. I don't like accepting compliments, so when I get a lot of them at once, I get a little antsy and awkward. So, I say hello, I let people be excited. I give hugs and take pictures, but it rarely gets much deeper than that. When it does start to get a little more personal, someone else is trying to make their way in or a tour manager ushers them away to make time for the next person.

In this video chatroom, I let myself linger a little more than is usually comfortable for me. The initial excitement and chatter calmed down, and everyone let each other speak. I got to hear their stories. I got to hear how much my music impacted them, when and how it found its way to them. Someone said, "Every time you put out a song, it's like you're talking about what I'm going through at that same time in my life," and the entire chat nodded and agreed in unison. People were quoting my old Vines the way I used to quote old commercials and YouTube videos. They told me they found each other through my music. Wow.

Wow.

I was able to gain access to a perspective, a world I've always been shielded from. I felt like a fly on a wall, like I was given an exclusive look into something that most artists don't get to experience. For the first time, I had a true understanding of the impact of my words and content.

It was so special and magical, and it reminded me why I do what I do, why I started all of this. I'm catering to the people who remind me of myself back then. I just want to be a safe place, a space to be yourself and find others who like you just as you come, who choose you for you.

It brought me back. It humbled me. It reminded me, after resenting the internet for so long, why I loved it in the first place. I miss making friends online. It feels like I'm only allowed to be friends with people if they have a following, or else I'm in some way "taking advantage" or "manipulating." I'm so tired of having to police every word I say because I know millions of other people are. I hate that having personal conversations about my life, that venting and sharing my stories, has become something to be criticized.

You are all people. I have always seen you as just that. Other people, looking for friends in an alternate universe that feels safer than our own. It's not safe for me anymore; I'm so glad it still is for you.

Thank you for finding me. I am very grateful I found you.

ABOUT THE AUTHOR

Gabbie Hanna is the *New York Times* bestselling author and illustrator of *Adultolescence* and a Billboard-charting musical artist. Starting off as a web-based creator, she amassed a combined 20 million followers across her social media platforms as she worked on her writing and music. A native of a small town in Pennsylvania and a University of Pittsburgh graduate, Gabbie shocked her loved ones when she drove cross-country to pursue her dreams in Los Angeles, where she currently resides. For more information, visit her @gabbiehanna on social media and gabbiehannaofficial.com.